D0119066

The story of Rudolph the Red-Nosed Reindeer is as magical as Christmas itself. Did you know that Rudolph began his career at Montgomery Ward? It's true.

The year was 1939, and Montgomery Ward advertising copywriter Robert L. May was hard at work on new Christmas ideas for children. Then one day he thought to himself, "What about a reindeer with a shiny red nose who helps Santa deliver presents on Christmas Eve?" It was as simple as that—Rudolph the Red-Nosed Reindeer was born.

Montgomery Ward was just the beginning for Rudolph. From there, he achieved even greater fame. Singer and cowboy movie star Gene Autry immortalized him in a song in 1949. In 1964, Rudolph starred in his very own television program, now a Christmas classic and a favorite of children of all ages. And in 1991, Robert L. May's daughter discovered, in an unopened box of her father's things, *Rudolph's Second Christmas*, a story written by her father in 1947 but never published.

Montgomery Ward is proud to bring you, for the very first time, Robert May's newly discovered sequel to the original classic Rudolph story.

RUDOLPH'S SECOND CHRISTMAS

RUDOLPH'S
SECOND CHRISTMAS
by Robert L. May
(Author of *Rudolph the Red-Nosed Reindeer*)

Illustrated by Michael Emberley

APPLEWOOD BOOKS
Distributed by The Globe Pequot Press
1992

Acknowledgements

The publisher would like to thank Mrs. Davies' first grade class at the Lt. Eleazor Davis School in Bedford, Massachusetts for their help in publishing this book.

The illustrator would like to thank Jennifer Pulver, whose skilled hands helped bring Rudolph back to life and whose patient heart helped bring me back to health.

© 1951 Robert L. May Co.

ISBN: 1-55709-192-7

FIRST EDITION

Thank you for purchasing an Applewood Book.
Applewood reprints America's lively classics—books from the past which are still of interest to modern readers—subjects such as cooking, gardening, money, travel, nature, sports, and history. Applewood Books are distributed by The Globe Pequot Press of Old Saybrook, CT. For a free copy of our current catalog, please write to Applewood Books, c/o The Globe Pequot Press, 6 Business Park Rd., P.O. Box 833, Old Saybrook, CT 06475-0833.

10 9 8 7 6 5 4 3 2 1

Library of Congress Cataloging in Publication Data
May, Robert Lewis, 1905-1976
    Rudolph's second Christmas / by Robert L. May : illustrated by Michael Emberley. – 1st ed.
        p.   cm.
    Summary: When Santa and Rudolph the Red-nosed Reindeer find a letter from two children who were forgotten the previous Christmas, Rudolph comes to their rescue and saves the day.
      ISBN 1-55709-192-7 : $9.95
      [1. Christmas–Fiction. 2. Reindeer–Fiction. 3. Santa Claus–Fiction.]
      I. Emberley, Michael, ill. II. Title.
    PZ7.M455Rv   1992
    [E]–dc20
                                     92-18416
                                     CIP
                                     AC

Remember Rudolph the Red-Nosed
Reindeer's first exciting Christmas?
Remember how his red, shining nose showed
Santa the way through the dark and foggy
Christmas Eve sky?

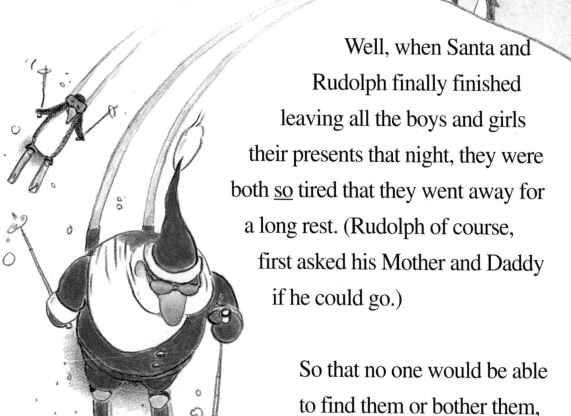

Well, when Santa and
Rudolph finally finished
leaving all the boys and girls
their presents that night, they were
both <u>so</u> tired that they went away for
a long rest. (Rudolph of course,
first asked his Mother and Daddy
if he could go.)

So that no one would be able
to find them or bother them,
they went as <u>far</u> from Santa's
North Pole office as they could...way
down to the South Pole.

After a three week rest, Santa took Rudolph
back to his Mother and
Daddy. Then Santa went back
to his own North Pole office.

He unlocked the front
door and pushed,

but the door hardly budged.

Then he backed up,

took a running start,

and crashed his big, round tummy against
the door, just as hard as he could.

Santa bounced off, like a big
round rubber ball.
The door moved a little this time,
just enough for Santa to squeeze in.

And there he found the whole room filled to the
ceiling with letters the mailman had dropped
through the mail-slot while Santa'd been
away...letters written by children to
thank Santa for their presents.
"How will I <u>ever</u> be able to read
them," cried Santa. "With just
one small lamp in my office,
and the North Pole night
six months long, I'll
ruin my eyes.

If only Rudolph were here to
help me, and to light-up the
room with his shining red
nose! <u>There's</u> an idea!
I'll <u>phone</u> him."

So Santa sent for Rudolph, who came right away, sat down next to Santa, and helped him open and read those piles and piles of letters.

Suddenly Santa heard...

Rudolph was crying...

"Here Santa, you read this letter,
Before my tears make the words any wetter."

Dear Santa,
You didn't find us, Christmas
Eve, because Daddy's circus moves
to a different town every day

so Our stockings were empty
christmas morning we didn't get any
PRESENTS AT ALL. PLEASE, SANTA, TRY
HARD TO FIND US NEXT CHRISTMAS, cause Mother
and Daddy say we've been very, very good.

with love,
Sonny
and
SIS

Then Rudolph said to Santa:

"We'll have to find out where their circus will be.

And the very best person to find them...is me!"

So Rudolph traveled to the town where Sonny's and Sis's letter had been mailed. Meeting some boys and girls, Rudolph asked if they knew where the circus was.

"That silly little circus? It left for the next town <u>weeks</u> ago."

"It only stayed here one day." ·

"Nobody went to see it."

"It was <u>terrible</u>."

The same thing happened in the next town. And the next. And the next. And, 10 towns later, when Rudolph finally caught-up with "that silly little circus," he quickly understood why <u>no</u> town would let it stay for more than one day.

The circus band, instead of playing the way circus bands <u>should</u>...played like this:

Instead of lions and tigers that roared real loud...they had just one toothless old tiger who didn't scare <u>anyone</u>.

And instead of shooting a man from a cannon, they shot a tiny mouse from a pop-gun!

"No wonder no one buys tickets," Sonny said
sadly to Rudolph.

"By next Christmas, Rudolph," cried Sis, "we don't know
<u>where</u> we'll be! So you and Santa may not find us <u>next</u>
Christmas either."

You can easily see why Rudolph felt sadder than ever when he left Sonny and Sis and the circus, and started his long trip back to the North Pole.

That evening, while going through a dark forest and looking for a place to sleep, Rudolph heard noises he felt quite sure must be animals...

When Rudolph got close enough to shine his red nose on them, was he surprised!

The sound of an animal running very fast...was a
turtle...another walking very, very slowly...a rabbit! The barking came from a cat...the meows from a dog. The
singing bird was a parrot...and the talking bird a canary.
 (And <u>none</u> of them looked very happy.)

Rudolph looked at the animals and said:
"You all look so sad, and you all look so queer...
Excuse me for staring...but why are you here?"

"I'm the best talker here," the canary said to Rudolph. "So I'll try to tell you why we're here. You can't really <u>expect</u> us to look happy. After all, each of us has been stared at and laughed at and teased, ever since we were babies. Just because we're a little

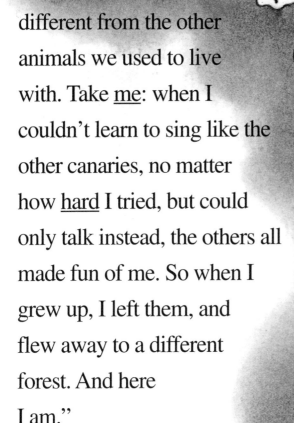

different from the other animals we used to live with. Take <u>me</u>: when I couldn't learn to sing like the other canaries, no matter how <u>hard</u> I tried, but could only talk instead, the others all made fun of me. So when I grew up, I left them, and flew away to a different forest. And here I am."

Rudolph then learned from the canary how the parrot had come to this forest for almost the same reason:— it had never learned to say "Polly want a cracker," like the smarter parrots, but could only just sing.

The dog that said "meow" had been teased and barked at by the rest of the dogs.

Because the barking cat sounded just like a dog,
she couldn't help frightening all the other cats,
who would run up the nearest tree when they heard her.

The slow-walking rabbit could never keep up with his fast-moving friends.

And whenever the fast-running turtle tried to slow-up to wait for the others, he would trip and land on his back. (And you probably know how hard it is for an upside down turtle to get on his <u>feet</u> again!)

So each of these little animals had been sad and lonely, laughed at and teased. Even after they had all come together in the forest, they were <u>still</u> a little sad and a little lonesome. (But at least they didn't tease or laugh at each other. After all, there was <u>something</u> a bit peculiar about <u>each</u> of them!)

"As a matter of fact," the canary said to Rudolph, "You're a little different from other Reindeer, too! Why don't you stay here with us? After all, isn't your nose a little bit, er... a little er..."

Rudolph smiled and said,

"You can't hurt my feelings; my nose is a sight..
But it sure helped old Santa, that dark, foggy night!

I know how it feels to be teased just like you
But I've an idea. I know what I'll do

To make each of you just as happy as me.
So first I'll tell Santa. Then, boy! Wait and see!"

Can you guess what Rudolph's wonderful idea was?

Yes, by Christmas that year, the "silly little circus" had become the grandest in the whole wide world! All because of Rudolph's idea...

Sonny and Sis's parents
were happy, because they had a circus everyone
wanted to see. All the boys and girls were so
happy to see this great circus that it wasn't able to
leave that town for ten whole months. Santa and Rudolph
were happy, too, because they knew that this year they
would have no trouble finding Sonny and Sis and filling
 their stockings all the way to the top.

Sonny and Sis were happy, because this year Santa brought them everything they asked for. In fact he brought each of them an extra present because of having missed them the year before.

And when it was all over, Santa said, "Rudolph, you've made as many people happy on this your second Christmas with me, as you did on your first."

Rudolph felt very proud, and he said...

"I hope you'll invite me to help you each year.
The happiest moment allowed any deer

Is riding with you, sir, and guiding your sleigh
(The number-one job on the number-one day)

And calling to all, as we drive out of sight:—

MERRY CHRISTMAS TO ALL,
AND TO ALL
A GOOD NIGHT!"